> Dedicated to those
> who must always win and
> who are never wrong.

Copyright © 2022 The Hastings Family

All rights reserved. No portion of this book may be reproduced in any form without permission from the publisher, except as permitted by U.S. copyright law. For permissions contact: susan.hastings@gmail.com

# Message from the Family

This book is a celebration of Chuck "Peewee" Hastings' love of treats and his enthusiasm for sharing his favorite sweets with family, friends, new acquaintances, and even strangers. Peewee inherited his passion for cookies from his mother, Ruth...Grandma Hastings! When Grandma Hastings was in town, the cookie jar was always full of homemade cookies. Peewee continued his mother's legacy and each Christmas made some of Grandma Hastings' specialties to share with friends.

In the early years, there were consistent classics like Buckeyes, Snickerdoodles, and Crystal Cut Candy, but he would also strike out and try something new each year. At first, Peewee's cookies were served when you came over to the house, or he would bring a small plate with a sampling as a gift when he visited someone for dinner. Over time, friends and neighbors began making special requests for a specific cookie or treat. Eager not to disappoint, Peewee made note of individual preferences and ensured that each friend got their fill of their favorite. Now, just like Santa Claus, Peewee has a list and he checks it twice.

Cookie season begins in November, and Peewee hands out platters of cookies to friends near and far. Yes, he even ships cookies across the country! While Peewee's cookies are a holiday staple, they are also a welcome surprise throughout the year for a few.

Peewee is also a fantastic mixologist and entertains his guests with perfectly mixed martinis! His famous martini recipes, and even a few other specialties, are also included in this book.

This book and its publication was Peewee's birthday gift in 2022. We hope you enjoy everything it has to offer and we enthusiastically endorse the recipes that fill its pages.

With Love,
The Hastings' Family

# Table of Contents

## Cookies & Treats

2. Almost No-Bake Mini Chocolate Peanut Butter Pies
3. Bourbon Balls
4. Buck Eyes
5. Chocolate Cherry Blossom Cookies
6. Chocolate Chip Cookies
7. Christmas Holly
8. Coconut Macaroons
9. Cracker Candy
10. Cranberry Pecan Oatmeal Cookies
11. Crystal Cut Candy
12. Fudge
13. Giant Molasses Cookies
14. Haystacks
15. Miracle Bars (aka 7-Layer Magic Bars)
16. Oatmeal Scotchies
17. Reese's Peanut Butter Cupcakes
18. Republican Cookies
19. Snickerdoodles
20. Steamed Cranberry Pudding
21. Truffles - Oreo
22. Truffles - Samoa

# Table of Contents

## Martinis

- 24   Almond Joy
- 25   Carmel 'Tini
- 26   Chocolate Martini
- 27   Kumquat Martini
- 28   Lavender Martini

## Other Goodies

- 30   Beef Stick
- 31   Hearty Breakfast Egg Bake
- 32   Pea Salad

# Almost No-Bake Mini Chocolate Peanut Butter Pies

Chocolate Peanut Butter Pie made even more drool worthy with perfect proportions in individual mini pie form! These Mini Chocolate Peanut Butter Pies are an easy, make ahead, almost no bake rich, decadently DELICIOUS dessert with a toffee graham cracker crust, creamy peanut butter filling, and silky chocolate ganache topping sure to satisfy all your peanut butter, chocolate cravings. They are made ahead and freeze so they are the ideal stress free entertaining or special occasion dessert!

| Prep Time | 25 minutes |
|---|---|
| Cook Time | 7 minutes |
| Servings | 12 |

## INGREDIENTS

### Graham Cracker Toffee Crust

- 5 whole graham cracker sheets
- 3 tablespoons unsalted butter, melted
- 1 tablespoon brown sugar
- 2 tablespoons toffee bits (I use Heath Bits 'O Brickle Toffee bits)

### Peanut Butter Pie Filling

- 1 cup heavy cream
- 6 oz. cream cheese, room temperature
- 1 cup smooth peanut butter
- 1 cup confectioners' sugar
- 1/2 cup toffee bits (I use Heath Bits 'O Brickle Toffee bits)
- 2 teaspoons vanilla extract
- 1/4 teaspoon salt

### Chocolate Ganache

- 4 oz. quality semisweet chocolate, chopped, Bakers, Guittard or Ghirardelli. Other brands have too many additives and will not melt nicely.
- 1/2 cup heavy cream

### Garnish

- 1/4 cup chopped salted peanuts
- 1 1/2 tablespoons smooth peanut butter
- mini chocolate chips (optional)
- chopped peanut butter cups (optional)

*www.carlsbadcravings.com

## INSTRUCTIONS

1. Preheat oven to 350F. Line a 12-count regular size muffin tin with muffin/cupcake liners.
2. Add Graham Cracker Crust ingredients to food processor and blend to a fine crumble. Divide Crust mixture between the 12 liners (about a heaping tablespoon each) and press into the bottom of the liners. Bake for 5-7 minutes or until lightly golden. Set aside.
3. Add heavy cream to a large mixing bowl and beat with handheld electric mixer on high until firm peaks form. Set aside.
4. To a separate mixing bowl (or remove heavy cream), using the same beaters, beat peanut butter and cream cheese until smooth. Add the confectioners' sugar, toffee bits, vanilla, and salt and beat until smooth (it will be thick). Gently fold the whipped heavy cream into the peanut butter-cream cheese mixture with a spatula until completely blended.
5. Spoon Peanut Butter Pie Filling into muffin tins (they will fill to the top). Freeze for at least one hour.
6. Meanwhile, prepare Chocolate Ganache by microwaving heavy cream for approximately 90 seconds until hot but not boiling. Add chopped chocolate and let sit one minute then whisk vigorously until smooth. Let cool to barely warm, stirring occasionally (it will thicken as it cools.). Spoon the Chocolate Ganache over the peanut butter cups and spread with the back of the spoon (it's okay if some spreads over the edges).
7. To garnish, melt peanut butter and drizzle over mini pies (I add my peanut butter to a Ziploc bag and snip the corner), sprinkle with salted peanuts and mini chocolate chips. Freeze for at least 4 hours up to 7 days. (See Notes)
8. When ready to serve, serve IMMEDIATELY after removing from the freezer as the mini pies soften quickly. You can either serve with or without the cupcake liners.

## RECIPE NOTES

**When to Garnish**: You can garnish your Chocolate Peanut Butter Pies either after you have spooned your ganache over the pies and the chocolate has set (it should set in about 5 minutes at room temperature) or freeze the pies after the ganache, then garnish and freeze again. I don't recommend garnishing right before serving because you will want the pies to firm up again after sitting at room temperature while you garnish.

It is also optional if you garnish with or without the wrappers. I like to keep the wrappers on for the ganache, so it doesn't spill over the sides and then remove the wrappers, place pies on a baking sheet and proceed to garnish, then freeze. There really isn't a right or wrong though, just as long as you freeze the pies after you garnish.

# Bourbon Balls

## Bourbon Balls

*Very good Dec 86*

- 2 12-ounce boxes vanilla wafers, finely ground
- 1 1-pound bag shelled pecans, finely chopped
- ½ pound confectioners' sugar (1¾ cups)
- 1 12-ounce package semi-sweet chocolate bits
- ½ cup white corn syrup
- 1½ cups bourbon (more or less for proper consistency)

Mix the wafers, pecans and confectioners' sugar in a large bowl. In a separate pan, over low heat, melt the chocolate bits. Add syrup and mix well. Add bourbon to chocolate-syrup mix; combine well and add to first mixture. Cover and let stand several hours or overnight.

Shape into 1-inch balls and roll in confectioners' sugar. Place in layers (separated with plastic wrap) in a tightly covered metal or plastic container. Let stand at least 12 hours before serving. Balls keep well for 4 or 5 weeks.

Yield: About 7 dozen.

*Dec 83 - very good; Paul Klavity loves it.*

**Half Recipe:**
- 2 cups crushed vanilla wafers
- 2 cups finely chopped pecans
- 1 cup xxx sugar
- 4 Table cocoa powder
- ½ cup Bourbon (or Rum)
- 2 Table KARO syrup.

Follow same instructions as above, except mix the COCOA powder w/ dry ingredients.

# Buck Eyes

Recipe for **Buck Eyes**

From the kitchen of **Ruth Hastings**   Serves ___
A favorite of **Debbie F, Shirley C, everyone**
Ingredients:
- 1 # butter
- 2 # peanut butter - creamy
- 3 # XXX sugar
- 1 Large bag choc. chips

Mix all with a mixer, then by hand. Roll into little balls, chill. Dip into melted chocolate chips. Set on waxed paper to harden. Store in the refrigerator.

Oven/Range directions

To halve the recipe
- 1/2 # butter = 2 4oz sticks
- 1 lb Peanut Butter
- 5.5 cups XXX

Microwave instructions

1# XXX = 3 3/4 C

# Chocolate Cherry Blossom Cookies

Peanut Blossoms are a favorite of so many households (including ours!). I would never dream of going a Christmas without them!

I don't think it's possible to improve on the original. However, this version tastes amazing and looks so festive! Serve them alongside your traditional blossoms for a colorful looking cookie tray!

## Chocolate Cherry Blossom Cookies

Author: Krystle
Prep time: 20 mins     Cook time: 12 mins     Total time: 32 mins

### Ingredients

- 1 Cup (2 Sticks) Butter, Softened
- 1 Cup Powdered Sugar
- 2 Teaspoons Maraschino Cherry Liquid
- Red Food Coloring (I used Gel)
- ½ Teaspoon Vanilla Extract
- 2¼ Cups All Purpose Flour
- 10 Oz. Jar Maraschino Cherries
- 3 Tablespoons White Sugar
- 36 Hershey's Kisses, Unwrapped

Order Ingredients

See A Christmas Squash Casserole Recipe

### Instructions

1. Preheat oven to 325 degrees Fahrenheit.
2. Drain cherries of their liquid, but be sure to reserve ~2 Teaspoons of their juice.
3. Cream butter using a mixer or wooden spoon. Gradually stir in powdered sugar a little at a time.
4. Stir in cherry juice, red food coloring, and vanilla
5. Gradually stir in flour a little at a time. Mix until just combined.
6. Fold in cherries.
7. Shape dough into ~1 inch balls. Roll in white sugar. Gently flatten using a small juice glass.
8. Bake 12-15 minutes, or until the sides are just beginning to brown. Remove from oven and immediately press a kiss into the middle of each cookie.

*www.bakingbeauty.net

# Chocolate Chip Cookies

*These are good*

### Chocolate Chip Cookies at Their Best

- 1 cup (½ lb.) butter or margarine, at room temperature
- ½ cup solid vegetable shortening
- 1½ cups granulated sugar
- 1 cup firmly packed brown sugar
- 4 large eggs
- 1 tablespoon vanilla
- 1 teaspoon lemon juice
- 3 cups all-purpose flour
- 2 teaspoons baking soda
- 1½ teaspoons salt
- 1 teaspoon ground cinnamon (optional)
- ½ cup rolled oats
- 2 large packages (12 oz. *each*) semisweet chocolate baking chips
- 2 cups chopped walnuts

In large bowl of an electric mixer, beat butter, shortening, granulated sugar, and brown sugar on high speed until very light and fluffy, about 5 minutes. Add eggs, one at a time, beating well after each addition. Beat in vanilla and lemon juice. In another bowl, stir together flour, baking soda, salt, cinnamon, and oats. Gradually add to butter mixture, blending thoroughly. Stir in chocolate and walnuts.

Use a scant ¼ cup of dough for each cooky. Drop dough onto lightly greased baking sheets, spacing cookies about 3 inches apart.

For soft cookies, bake in a 325° oven until light golden brown, 17 to 19 minutes; for crisp cookies, bake in a 350° oven until golden brown, 16 to 18 minutes. Transfer to racks to cool. Serve, or store airtight. Makes about 3 dozen.

# Christmas Holly

# Coconut Macaroons

*A light and airy cookie that's crispy on the outside and chewy on the inside.*

- 2 egg whites
- ½ teaspoon vanilla
- ⅔ cup sugar
- 1 3½-ounce can (1⅓ cups) flaked coconut

Oven 325°

In a mixing bowl beat egg whites and vanilla till soft peaks form (tips curl). Gradually add sugar, beating till stiff peaks form (tips stand straight). Fold in coconut. Drop by rounded teaspoons 2 inches apart onto a greased cookie sheet. Bake in a 325° oven about 20 minutes or till edges are lightly browned. Cool cookies on a wire rack. Makes about 30.

**Nutty Macaroons:** Prepare as above, except add ½ cup chopped toasted *almonds, pecans,* or *hazelnuts (filberts)* with the coconut.

**Lemon Macaroons:** Prepare as above, except substitute 1 tablespoon *lemon juice* for the vanilla and add 1 teaspoon finely shredded *lemon peel* with the coconut.

# Cracker Candy

## CRACKER CANDY

Line cookie sheet with foil. Arrange 40 saltine crackers in pan.

Cook: *Spray w/ Pam*

1 c. brown sugar
1 c. butter
1 to 2 tsp vanilla

Optional: pecans or almonds

Bring sugar and butter to boil and cook 3 minutes, stirring constantly. Remove from the heat and add the vanilla. Pour over crackers and spread with a spoon. Bake at 400 degrees for about 5 minutes. Watch closely to make sure it does not burn. Remove from oven and sprinkle on one 12 ounce *(2c)* package of chocolate chips (I like Hersheys). Let stand to melt. **Spread** and refrigerate. Break apart and serve. Tastes a lot like Heath or Skor candy bars.

*A Susan favorite*

# Cranberry Pecan Oatmeal Cookies

☆☆☆☆☆ *www.greatgrubdelicioustreats.com

**Servings** 4 dozen
**Author** Terri

### Ingredients
- 1 cup butter 2 sticks, softened
- 1 cup brown sugar firmly packed
- ½ cup sugar
- 2 eggs
- 1 tsp vanilla
- 1½ cups flour
- 1 tsp baking soda
- 1 tsp cinnamon
- ½ tsp salt
- 3 cups uncooked oats
- 1 cup fresh cranberries chopped into small pieces
- 1 cup pecans chopped
- 1 cup white chocolate chips

### Instructions
1. Preheat oven to 350°
2. Using a large mixing bowl, add butter and sugars and beat until creamy.
3. Mix in eggs and vanilla. Beat until well combined.
4. In a separate bowl, whisk flour, baking soda, cinnamon and salt.
5. Add flour mixture to large mixing bowl and mix well.
6. Stir in oatmeal then gently stir in cranberries, pecans and white chocolate chips.
7. Drop by rounded teaspoon onto ungreased cookie sheet.
8. Bake for approximately 10-12 minutes or until cookies start to brown around the edges.
9. Once removed from oven, place cookies on a wire rack to cool.

# Crystal Cut Candy

### CRYSTAL CUT CANDY

- 2 C Sugar
- ½ C Light Corn Syrup (Karo)
- ½ C Water
- Dash Salt
- 5-6 Drops Oil
- Food Coloring
- Powdered Sugar

Combine sugar, syrup, water and salt - stir until boil. Insert candy thermometer and heat to Hard Crack 290°. Remove from - turn on exhaust fan - add oil and appropriate food coloring. Pour mixture into 8"x 8" pan and allow to cool, where marks in mixture do not disappear and are not sticky to spatula. Keep marking candy in ½" squares until center is cool. Invert pan and strike down flat on wax paper. Crack candy into ½" squares using knife handle. Lightly dust with powdered sugar. — Reminder, when handling oil and candy, be sure and wash hands. Oil will burn face. Do not have face over hot mixture when stirring in oil and coloring; steam will burn face.

# Fudge

### Short-Cut Fudge

2 (7 oz) pkgs semi-sweet chocolate
1 1/3 c (15-oz can) condensed milk
1 tsp vanilla
1 c chopped nut meats

Melt chocolate in top of dbl boiler. Add condensed milk & stir until well blended. Remove from heat. Add vanilla & nut meats. Pour into pan which has been buttered or lined w/ wax paper. Chill for a few hours. When firm, cut into squares. Makes about 2 lbs.

# Giant Molasses Cookies

*2021 Rolled a little smaller & Baked for 10 min @ 350°*

## Ingredients

- 1-1/2 cups butter, softened
- 2 cups sugar
- 2 large eggs, room temperature
- 1/2 cup molasses
- 4-1/2 cups all-purpose flour
- 4 teaspoons ground ginger
- 2 teaspoons baking soda
- 1-1/2 teaspoons ground cinnamon
- 1 teaspoon ground cloves
- 1/4 teaspoon salt
- 1/4 cup chopped pecans
- 3/4 cup coarse sugar

## Directions

1. Preheat oven to 350°. In a large bowl, cream butter and sugar until light and fluffy. Beat in eggs and molasses. Combine the flour, ginger, baking soda, cinnamon, cloves and salt; gradually add to creamed mixture and mix well. Fold in pecans.

2. Shape into 2-in. balls and roll in coarse sugar. Place 2-1/2 in. apart on ungreased baking sheets. Bake 13-15 minutes or until tops are cracked. Remove to wire racks to cool.

### KITCHEN TIPS

- Molasses is a byproduct of refining cane or beets into sugar. Light and dark molasses are made from the first and second refining processes, respectively. Blackstrap, made from the third procedure, is the strongest, darkest and most intensely flavored of the three. Dark molasses works well in most recipes.
- For easy cleanup, spritz the measuring cup with a little cooking spray before measuring the sticky molasses.

*www.tasteofhome.com

# Haystacks

6 ounces of butterscotch morsels
2 teaspoons of vegetable oil
2 cups of chow mien noodles
2 cups of miniature marshmallows

In double boiler over hot boiling water, melt morsels. Stir in oil. In large bowl, mix chow mien noodles and marshmallows. Pour on butterscotch and mix thoroughly with a fork. Drop by heaping teaspoonfuls on a wax-paper lined cookie sheet and chill until set.

# Miracle Bars
## aka 7-Layer Magic Bars

- ½ cup margarine or butter
- 1½ cups graham cracker crumbs
- 1 (14-ounce) can Eagle® Brand Sweetened Condensed Milk (NOT evaporated milk)
- 1 cup (6 ounces) semi-sweet chocolate chips
- 1 (6-ounce) package butterscotch flavored chips
- 1 (3 ½-ounce) can flaked coconut (1 ⅓ cups)
- 1 cup chopped California walnuts

Preheat oven to 350° (325° for glass dish). In 13x9-inch baking pan, melt margarine in oven. Sprinkle crumbs over margarine; pour Eagle® Brand evenly over crumbs. Top with remaining ingredients in order listed; press down firmly. Bake 25 to 30 minutes or until lightly browned. Cool. Chill if desired. Cut into bars. Store loosely covered at room temperature.

# Oatmeal Scotchies

## OATMEAL SCOTCHIES

Preheat oven to 375°F. In small bowl, combine 1 cup flour, 1 teasp. baking powder, ½ teasp. baking soda and ½ teasp. salt; set aside. In large bowl, combine ½ cup butter, softened, ¾ cup firmly packed brown sugar, 1 egg and 1½ teasps. water; beat until creamy. Gradually add flour mixture. Stir in ¾ cup quick oats, uncooked, one 6-oz. pkg. (1 cup) NESTLÉ BUTTERSCOTCH MORSELS and ¼ teasp. orange extract. Drop by slightly rounded measuring tablespoonfuls onto greased cookie sheets.
BAKE at: 375°F.   TIME: 10-12 minutes   Makes 2 dozen 3" cookies

*Very good!! Dec 77 - out this - remove to cool ASAP*

*Dec 78 melted butter 1 cup Oatmeal*

16

# Reese's Peanut Butter Cupcakes

Serves: 16

**Ingredients**

- *Cupcakes:*
- 1 15.2 ounce chocolate cake mix
- 2 eggs
- 1 cup sour cream (NOT low fat)
- ½ cup milk
- 1/3 cup vegetable oil
- 32-40 Reese's mini peanut butter cups, unwrapped
- *Peanut Butter Frosting*
- 1 stick of butter (1/2 cup) room temperature
- ½ cup peanut butter
- 4 cups powdered sugar
- 1 teaspoon vanilla
- 3 Tablespoons milk (or more as needed)

*½ frosting quantities*

**Instructions**

1. Preheat oven to 350 degrees and line cupcake pans with paper/foil liners.
2. For the cupcakes: Combine the cake mix, eggs, sour cream, milk, and vegetable oil in a large bowl until incorporated. Scrape sides of bowl and then beat on medium high speed for 3 minutes.
3. Fill cupcake liners halfway full and press one peanut butter cup into the center of each. Add additional tablespoon of batter over the top of the peanut butter cup. Bake for 13 to 15 min., or until a toothpick inserted into the side comes out just a tad crumbly. Cool
4. For the frosting; In a mixing bowl, cream butter and peanut butter until fluffy. Add the powdered sugar, vanilla, and milk and continue creaming until well blended. Beat on low speed until moistened, beat on medium high until frosting is fluffy. Add more milk, or confectioners sugar until you reach a nice thick frosting.
5. Pipe frosting onto cupcakes. I cut a small corner out of a gallon Ziploc bag, and put all frosting in that. Cut remaining peanut butter cups in half, and put on top of frosting.

*Put small amount of batter in each cup, and place PB cup on top, fill around and over the PB cup. If PB cup is pushed down the cupcake collapses.*

www.tastesbetterfromscratch.com

# Republican Cookies

**TX Governor's Mansion Cowboy Cookies (Republican Cookies)** 350°

- 1 C Butter @ room temp
- 1 C Granulated Sugar
- 1 C Brown Sugar
- 2 Eggs
- 2 Tsp Vanilla
- 2 C Flour
- 2 Tsp Baking Powder
- 2 Tsp Ground Cinnamon
- 2/3 Tsp Salt
- 2 C Choc Chips
- 2 C Old Fashioned Oats
- 1 1/3 C Sweetened Flaked Coconut
- 1 1/3 C Chopped Pecans
- 2 Tsp Baking Soda

Mix flour, baking powder, baking soda, cinnamon & salt together.

Beat softened butter @ med speed until smooth & creamy. Gradually beat in sugars. Add eggs one at a time. Beat in vanilla.

Stir in flour mixture until just combined. Next add oats, choc chips, coconut & pecans that have been combined.

Drop heaping tsp of dough on ungreased cookie sheet. Bake 10-15 minutes or until edges are lightly browned.

# Snickerdoodles

400°

SNICKERDOODLES

1 C soft shortening  
1½ C sugar  } mix together thoroughly
2 eggs

2¾ c sifted flour  
2 TSP cream of tartar  } sift together & stir in
1 TSP soda  
½ TSP salt

Chill dough. Roll into balls the size of small walnuts. Roll in mixture of 2 TBSP sugar, ½ TSP cinnamon. Place about 2-inch apart on ungreased cooky sheet. Bake 8-10 min (400°) until lightly browned.

COOKIES!

19

# Steamed Cranberry Pudding

## STEAMED CRANBERRY PUDDING

- 2 C Cranberries
- 1 1/3 C Flour
- 1/2 Tsp Salt
- 1/4 Tsp Cinnamon
- 1/4 Tsp Cloves
- 1/4 Tsp Mace
- 2 Tsp Baking Soda
- 1/3 C Hot Water
- 1/2 C Molasses

Halve cranberries, add to flour, salt, spices & soda. Combine hot water & molasses, then blend with first mixture. Transfer to well greased double boiler. Cover & steam for 2 1/2 hours.
(Toffee Sauce on Reverse)

## Toffee Sauce

Combine 1 C Sugar, 1 C canned milk, 1/3 C butter in double boiler. Add 1/2 Tsp vanilla. Heat for minimum 1 Hour. — Serve warm.

# Oreo Truffles

Only 3 ingredients and they are delicious!

Recipe type: Dessert

## Ingredients

- 1 package Double Stuffed Oreos
- 4 oz Cream Cheese, you may add up to 8 oz, I just like the consistency best with 4 oz.
- Dipping Chocolate, almond bark is my favorite because it hardens faster and quicker and doesn't melt as easy as chocolate chips after it sets up.

## Instructions

1. Chop Oreos up finely in a food processor. Save some of the finely crushed Oreos for garnish later and set it aside. You don't need too much.
2. With hands (or a spoon, I just think hands are faster), mash softened cream cheese and crushed Oreos until well combined.
3. Roll into 1" balls and place on a wax covered cookie sheet. Put in freezer for 15 minutes.
4. While balls are in freezer, melt chocolate according to directions.
5. Pull the Oreo Truffles out of freezer, and dip into chocolate. Garnish with reserved Oreo crumbs before the chocolate sets up.
6. Let chocolate set, refrigerate and enjoy!

For those that were wondering what kind of chocolate I used, here is a picture of mine. I used about half of the package. I followed the microwave instructions. I used a small but tall bowl to dip them in so that the entire truffle could easily be covered and carefully lifted it out with a fork (you can use skewers as well) and tapped my fork on the side to let any excess chocolate drip off. It is ideal to cover them with chocolate right after they have sat in the freezer for at least 15 minutes. The cold helps the chocolate set up faster.

*www.chef-in-training.com

# Samoa Truffles

Only FIVE ingredients and they couldn't be more delicious! Could be my favorite truffle yet!

Recipe type: Dessert

## Ingredients

- 1 (14.3 oz) package Golden Oreos
- 4 oz. softened cream cheese
- ¼ cup caramel topping
- 10 oz. chocolate candy coating
- ¼ cup toasted coconut

## Instructions

1. Finely crush oreos in a food processor and place fine crumbs in a medium bowl.
2. Add softened cream cheese and caramel topping to bowl. With hands (or a spoon, I just think hands are faster), mash softened cream cheese, caramel and crushed Oreos until well combined.
3. Roll into 1" balls and place on a wax covered cookie sheet. Put in freezer for 15 minutes.
4. While balls are in freezer, melt chocolate according to directions.
5. Pull the truffles out of freezer, and dip into chocolate one at a time. Try to remove as much excess chocolate as possible. Place back on wax paper on cookie sheet.
6. Immediately after placing chocolate dipped truffle on wax paper, garnish tops with toasted coconut before the chocolate sets up.
7. Let chocolate set, refrigerate and enjoy!

Oh my – sprinkle with a little SEA SALT on top for that extra TAH DAH !!

*www.chef-in-training.com

# Almond Joy

A derivative of the Chocolate Martini but **add**

2 Oz  Coconut Rum (Malibu)

Shake with a lot of ice, strain/pour and drink

> To spice this drink up, chop coconut flakes and place in plate.  In separate plate, chocolate syrup.  Dip rim of glass into the chocolate and then into the coconut.  Then pour refreshment into the glass.   Enjoy the Almond Joy.

# Carmel 'Tini

2 Oz  Vodka (Vanilla Vodka is smoother)
2 Oz  Pucker's Sour Apple Mix (or alternative one)
¾-1 Oz Butterscotch Schnapps (de Kuypers or alternative one)

Shake with a lot of ice, strain/pour and drink

If Sour Apple mix cannot be found, they make an Appletini mix that includes vodka, but the amount of vodka is so small, I treat the mix as if there is no vodka, as a sour apple substitute

# Chocolate Martini

2 Oz   Vodka (Vanilla Vodka is smoother)
2 Oz   Chocolate Liqueur (Trader Vic's is good, no need to go expensive)

You can drizzle chocolate along the inside of the glass or dip the rim into the chocolate on a plate (Hershey's Chocolate Syrup works well)

Shake with a lot of ice, strain/pour and drink

# Kumquat Martini

This easy-to-make and delicious recipe is from my friend Maggie Smith—the Aussie, not the British, actress. Use the greater amount of kumquats to intensify the citrus flavour. Cooking time does not reflect the months needed for the liqueur to age fully.

READY IN: 10mins

SERVES: 24

UNITS: US

## INGREDIENTS

**LIQUEUR**

- 15-30    kumquats, pricked
- 2 ¼      cups sugar (scant measure)
- 700      ml brandy

**COATING FOR LATER**

## DIRECTIONS

Put the pricked kumquats, sugar and brandy in a jar that can be tightly sealed (should hold at least a litre). Store jar away from sunlight.

Every day for the next 14 days, turn the jar over and back to distribute the sugar. You don't need to shake the jar.

After the 14 days are up, keep turning the jar over and back at least once a week until the sugar has completely dissolved.

When the sugar has dissolved, use tongs or a slotted spoon to gently remove the kumquats. Leave the liqueur to age in the jar.

Dip these boozy kumquats in melted chocolate for a delicious treat with after-dinner coffee. Store in the freezer.

Six months later, the liqueur is ready to be bottled and enjoyed. Maggie saves interesting-looking smaller bottles to use for gifts.

Note: You can bottle the liqueur at three months (to give as a gift), but tell the recipient it is worth waiting the extra three months before tasting. The well-aged liqueur is thicker, sweeter and more syrupy.

*www.food.com/recipe/maggies-lethal-kumquat-liqueur-271072

# Lavender Martini

2 Oz  Vodka (Vanilla Vodka is smoother)
1 Oz  Parfait Amour Liqueur (Marie Bizard's – hard to find, may have to substitute another purple liqueur like Crème de Violette, but the taste changes, so adjust lime juice and/or cranberry juice)
½ Oz  Rose's Lime Juice
2 Oz  White Cranberry Juice

Shake with a lot of ice, strain/pour and drink

# Beef Stick

In Large Plastic bowl with tight fitting lid---MIX

5 # hamburg (not ground chuck)
5 tsp Mortons Tender Quick Salt
2½ tsp garlic salt
2½ tsp coarse ground pepper
1 tbsp Hickory smoke salt (Spice Is. brand)
2½ tsp mustard seed

Mix well, cover and refrigerate.
2nd & 3rd day mix again and refrigerate.
4th day, shape into 5 rolls about 1½" X 10"
Spray broiler or cake racks with Pam, lay rolls on rack, put on bottom of oven rack.
150° for 8-10 hrs.
Store in ref. or freezer.

# Hearty Breakfast Egg Bake

★★★★½

*I always fix this casserole ahead of time when overnight guests are visiting so I have more time to spend with them. Then I simply add some toast or biscuits and fresh fruit for a complete meal that everyone loves. This dish also reheats well. —Pamela Norris, Fenton, Missouri*

**TOTAL TIME:** Prep: 10 min. + chilling Bake: 45 min. + standing
**YIELD:** 8 servings.

## Ingredients

1-1/2 pounds bulk pork sausage

3 cups frozen shredded hash brown potatoes, thawed

2 cups shredded cheddar cheese

8 large eggs, lightly beaten

1 can (10-3/4 ounces) condensed cream of mushroom soup, undiluted

3/4 cup evaporated milk

## Directions

1. Crumble sausage into a large skillet. Cook over medium heat until no longer pink; drain. Transfer to a greased 13x9-in. baking dish. Sprinkle with hash browns and cheese.

2. In a large bowl, whisk the remaining ingredients; pour over the top. Cover and refrigerate overnight.

3. Remove from the refrigerator 30 minutes before baking. Bake, uncovered, at 350° for 45-50 minutes or until a knife inserted in the center comes out clean. Let stand for 10 minutes before cutting.

© 2020 RDA Enthusiast Brands, LLC

*www.tasteofhome.com

# Pea Salad

*Thanksgiving 2021*

## Pea Salad

- 2 cans of canned peas
  - any kind
  - not frozen
- Cheddar cheese
  - a block of sharp or x-sharp cup into super small cubes
  - you have to see the cheese so that it's not insignificant, but not overwhelming.
- Dill pickles! 1½-2 large
  - <u>not</u> relish or sweet
  - cut up smaller than cheese: diced
- White onions
  - 4 slices super small like pickles or smaller
- Mix all together, then mix 2 heaping TBLS of Mayo to taste. The mayo is only to keep it together.

# Fun Tidbits

## Merry Christmas and Goodbye to 2020!

As you can see, I have been wearing my COOKIE SHIRT (thoughtfully given to me by my grandchildren), and YES, I've been baking!

As we leave 2020 behind us (good riddance) I thought you'd enjoy a few sweets to get you in the Holiday mood!

Your box has the following cookies and candies:

| | |
|---|---|
| Snicker Doodles | Cracker Candy And Fudge w/walnuts |
| Peanut Butter Balls/Buckeyes | Crystal Cut Candy – red & green |
| Butterscotch Haystacks | Holly Candy (yes, it is ALL edible) |
| Truffles – chocolate and caramel | Coconut Macaroons |
| Bourbon Balls | Republican (Texas) Cookies |
| Cherry Blossoms | Cranberry/Oatmeal and choc chip. |
| Miracle Bars | Oatmeal Scotchies |

Peewee's Organization

## 2020

- Holly (2)
- Haystacks (2)
- Cherry Blossoms
- Cracker Candy (3)
- Miracle Bars (2)
- Tx Mansion
- Cranberry Oatmeal Choc
- Oatmeal Scotchies (2)
- Snickerdoodles (2)
- Truffles
- Coconut Macaroons (2)
- Buck Eyes
- Bourbon Balls
- Fudge (2)
- Crystal Candy (4)

---

## 2020/2021

### Plates/Boxes     Mailings

**Mr. Charles Hastings**

| Plates/Boxes | Mailings |
|---|---|
| ✗ Rhonda + BB | ✗ Shirley Candy |
| ✗ Susan + | ✗ Tom/Maritza + |
| Julie | ✗ Becky + |
| Rosa – BB | Enid + |
| ✗ Veronica + Haystacks | ✗ Phyllis + |
| ✗ Mel/Sharon + BS | ✗ Ruth + |
| ✗ TJ/Tennyson + BS (8) | |
| ✗ Ron/Kim + BS | |
| ✗ Atoussa – BB | |
| ✗ Kimm/Mike + | |
| ✗ Sy/Barbara – BB | |
| ✗ Bob/Joan – BB | |
| ✗ Lisa/Guy (8) | |
| ✗ Suzanne + | |
| ✓ Aaron/Susan | |

10/13

CARIBBEAN PRINCESS

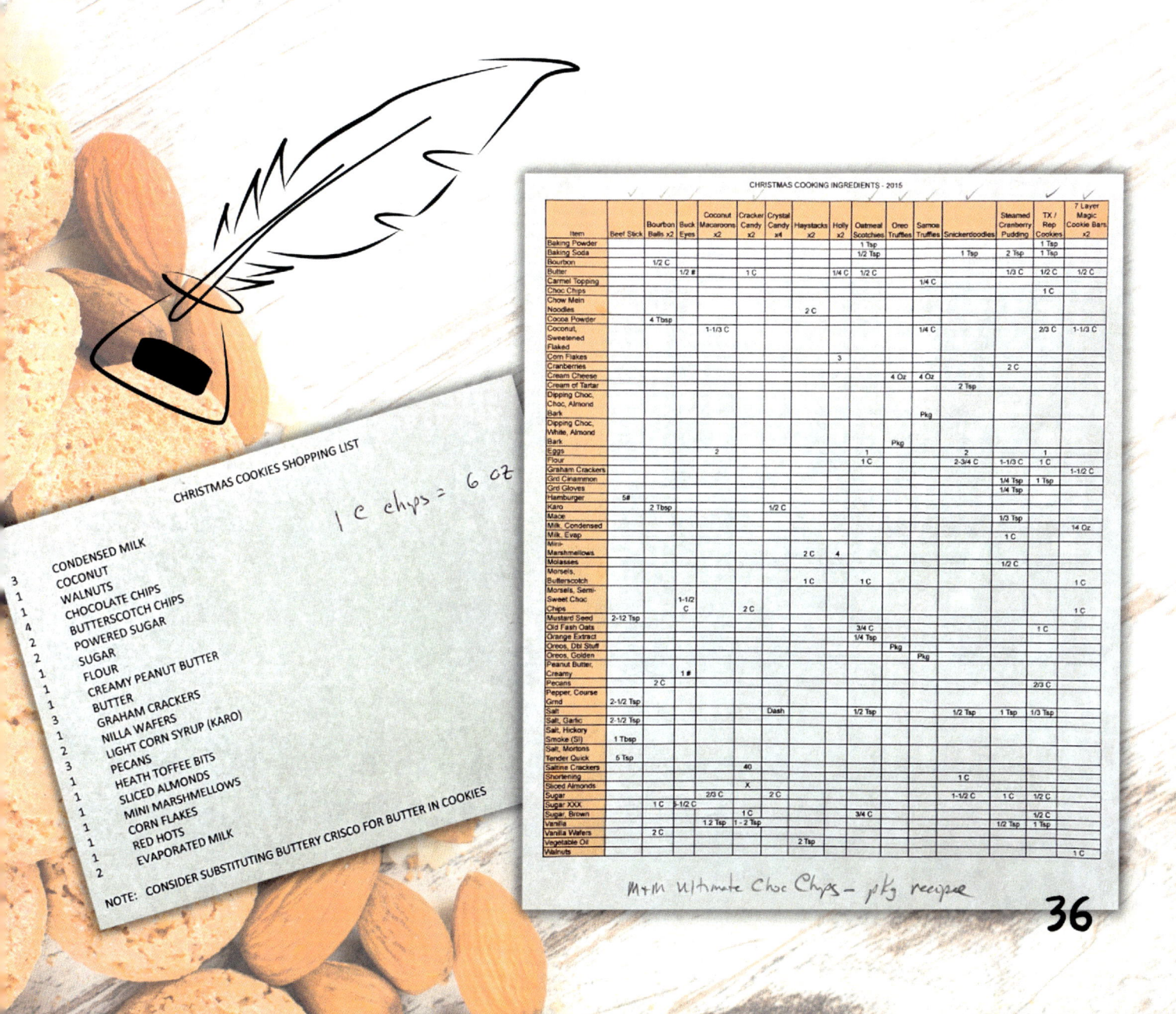

## CHRISTMAS COOKIES SHOPPING LIST

1 c chips = 6 oz

| Qty | Item |
|---|---|
| 3 | CONDENSED MILK |
|  | COCONUT |
| 1 | WALNUTS |
| 4 | CHOCOLATE CHIPS |
| 1 | BUTTERSCOTCH CHIPS |
|  | POWERED SUGAR |
| 2 | SUGAR |
| 1 | FLOUR |
|  | CREAMY PEANUT BUTTER |
| 1 | BUTTER |
| 3 | GRAHAM CRACKERS |
|  | NILLA WAFERS |
| 1 | LIGHT CORN SYRUP (KARO) |
| 2 | PECANS |
| 3 | HEATH TOFFEE BITS |
| 1 | SLICED ALMONDS |
| 1 | MINI MARSHMELLOWS |
| 1 | CORN FLAKES |
|  | RED HOTS |
| 1 | EVAPORATED MILK |
| 2 |  |

NOTE: CONSIDER SUBSTITUTING BUTTERY CRISCO FOR BUTTER IN COOKIES

## CHRISTMAS COOKING INGREDIENTS - 2015

| Item | Beef Stick | Bourbon Balls x2 | Buck Eyes | Coconut Macaroons x2 | Cracker Candy x4 | Crystal Candy | Haystacks x2 | Holly x2 | Oatmeal Scotchies | Oreo Truffles | Samoa Truffles | Snickerdoodles | Steamed Cranberry Pudding | TX / Rep Cookies | 7 Layer Magic Cookie Bars x2 |
|---|---|---|---|---|---|---|---|---|---|---|---|---|---|---|---|
| Baking Powder |  |  |  |  |  |  |  |  | 1 Tsp |  |  |  |  | 1 Tsp |  |
| Baking Soda |  |  |  |  |  |  |  |  | 1/2 Tsp |  |  | 1 Tsp | 2 Tsp | 1 Tsp |  |
| Bourbon |  | 1/2 C |  |  |  |  |  |  |  |  |  |  |  |  |  |
| Butter |  |  | 1/2 # |  | 1 C |  |  | 1/4 C | 1/2 C |  |  |  | 1/3 C | 1/2 C | 1/2 C |
| Carmel Topping |  |  |  |  |  |  |  |  |  |  | 1/4 C |  |  |  |  |
| Choc Chips |  |  |  |  |  |  |  |  |  |  |  |  |  | 1 C |  |
| Chow Mein Noodles |  |  |  |  |  |  | 2 C |  |  |  |  |  |  |  |  |
| Cocoa Powder |  | 4 Tbsp |  |  |  |  |  |  |  |  |  |  |  |  |  |
| Coconut, Sweetened Flaked |  |  |  | 1-1/3 C |  |  |  |  |  | 1/4 C |  |  |  | 2/3 C | 1-1/3 C |
| Corn Flakes |  |  |  |  |  |  | 3 |  |  |  |  |  |  |  |  |
| Cranberries |  |  |  |  |  |  |  |  |  |  |  | 2 C |  |  |  |
| Cream Cheese |  |  |  |  |  |  |  |  |  | 4 Oz | 4 Oz |  |  |  |  |
| Cream of Tartar |  |  |  |  |  |  |  |  |  |  |  | 2 Tsp |  |  |  |
| Dipping Choc, Choc, Almond Bark |  |  |  |  |  |  |  |  |  | Pkg |  |  |  |  |  |
| Dipping Choc, White, Almond Bark |  |  |  |  |  |  |  | Pkg |  |  |  |  |  |  |  |
| Eggs |  |  | 2 |  |  |  |  | 1 |  | 2 |  |  | 1 |  |  |
| Flour |  |  |  |  |  |  |  |  | 1 C |  |  | 2-3/4 C | 1-1/3 C | 1 C |  |
| Graham Crackers |  |  |  |  |  |  |  |  |  |  |  |  |  |  | 1-1/2 C |
| Grd Cinammon |  |  |  |  |  |  |  |  |  |  |  | 1/4 C | 1 Tsp |  |  |
| Grd Gloves |  |  |  |  |  |  |  |  |  |  |  |  | 1/4 C |  |  |
| Hamburger | 5# |  |  |  |  |  |  |  |  |  |  |  |  |  |  |
| Karo |  | 2 Tbsp |  |  | 1/2 C |  |  |  |  |  |  |  |  |  |  |
| Mace |  |  |  |  |  |  |  |  |  |  |  |  | 1/3 Tsp |  |  |
| Milk, Condensed |  |  |  |  |  |  |  |  |  |  |  |  |  |  | 14 Oz |
| Milk, Evap |  |  |  |  |  |  |  |  |  |  |  |  | 1 C |  |  |
| Mini-Marshmellows |  |  |  |  |  |  | 2 C | 4 |  |  |  |  |  |  |  |
| Molasses |  |  |  |  |  |  |  |  |  |  |  |  | 1/2 C |  |  |
| Morsels, Butterscotch |  |  |  |  |  |  | 1 C |  | 1 C |  |  |  |  |  | 1 C |
| Morsels, Semi-Sweet Choc Chips |  |  | 1-1/2 C |  | 2 C |  |  |  |  |  |  |  |  |  | 1 C |
| Mustard Seed | 2-12 Tsp |  |  |  |  |  |  |  |  |  |  |  |  |  |  |
| Old Fash Oats |  |  |  |  |  |  |  |  | 3/4 C |  |  |  |  | 1 C |  |
| Orange Extract |  |  |  |  |  |  |  |  |  |  | 1/4 Tsp |  |  |  |  |
| Oreos, Dbl Stuff |  |  |  |  |  |  |  |  |  | Pkg |  |  |  |  |  |
| Oreos, Golden |  |  |  |  |  |  |  |  |  |  | Pkg |  |  |  |  |
| Peanut Butter, Creamy |  |  | 1 # |  |  |  |  |  |  |  |  |  |  |  |  |
| Pecans |  | 2 C |  |  |  |  |  |  |  |  |  |  |  | 2/3 C |  |
| Pepper, Course Grnd | 2-1/2 Tsp |  |  |  |  |  |  |  |  |  |  |  |  |  |  |
| Salt |  |  |  |  | Dash |  |  |  | 1/2 Tsp |  |  | 1/2 Tsp | 1 Tsp | 1/3 C |  |
| Salt, Garlic | 2-1/2 Tsp |  |  |  |  |  |  |  |  |  |  |  |  |  |  |
| Salt, Hickory Smoke (Sl) |  | 1 Tbsp |  |  |  |  |  |  |  |  |  |  |  |  |  |
| Salt, Mortons Tender Quick | 5 Tsp |  |  |  |  |  |  |  |  |  |  |  |  |  |  |
| Saltine Crackers |  |  |  |  | 40 |  |  |  |  |  |  |  |  |  |  |
| Shortening |  |  |  |  | X |  |  |  |  |  |  | 1 C |  |  |  |
| Sliced Almonds |  |  |  |  |  |  |  |  |  |  |  |  |  | 1 C |  |
| Sugar |  |  |  | 2/3 C |  | 2 C |  |  |  |  |  | 1-1/2 C |  |  |  |
| Sugar XXX |  |  | 1 C | 1-1/2 C |  |  |  |  |  |  |  |  |  |  |  |
| Sugar, Brown |  |  |  |  | 1 C |  |  |  | 3/4 C |  |  |  |  | 1/2 C |  |
| Vanilla |  |  |  |  | 1.2 Tsp | 1 - 2 Tsp |  |  |  |  |  |  | 1/2 Tsp | 1 Tsp |  |
| Vanilla Wafers |  | 2 C |  |  |  |  |  |  |  |  |  |  |  |  |  |
| Vegetable Oil |  |  |  |  |  |  |  |  |  |  |  | 2 Tsp |  |  |  |
| Walnuts |  |  |  |  |  |  |  |  |  |  |  |  |  |  | 1 C |

M+M Ultimate Choc Chips - pkg recipe

# Family Pictures

37

38

39

40

41

42

43

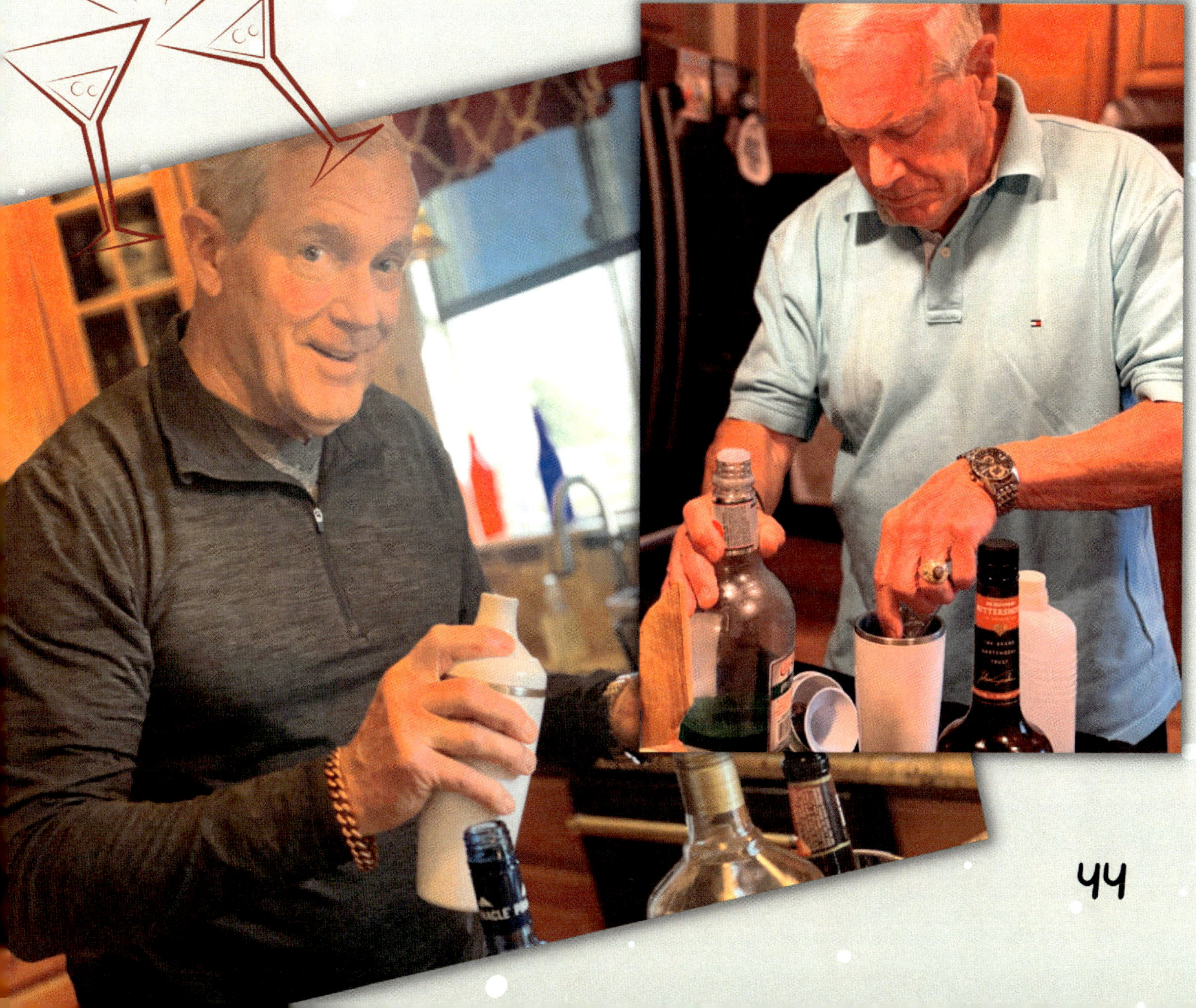

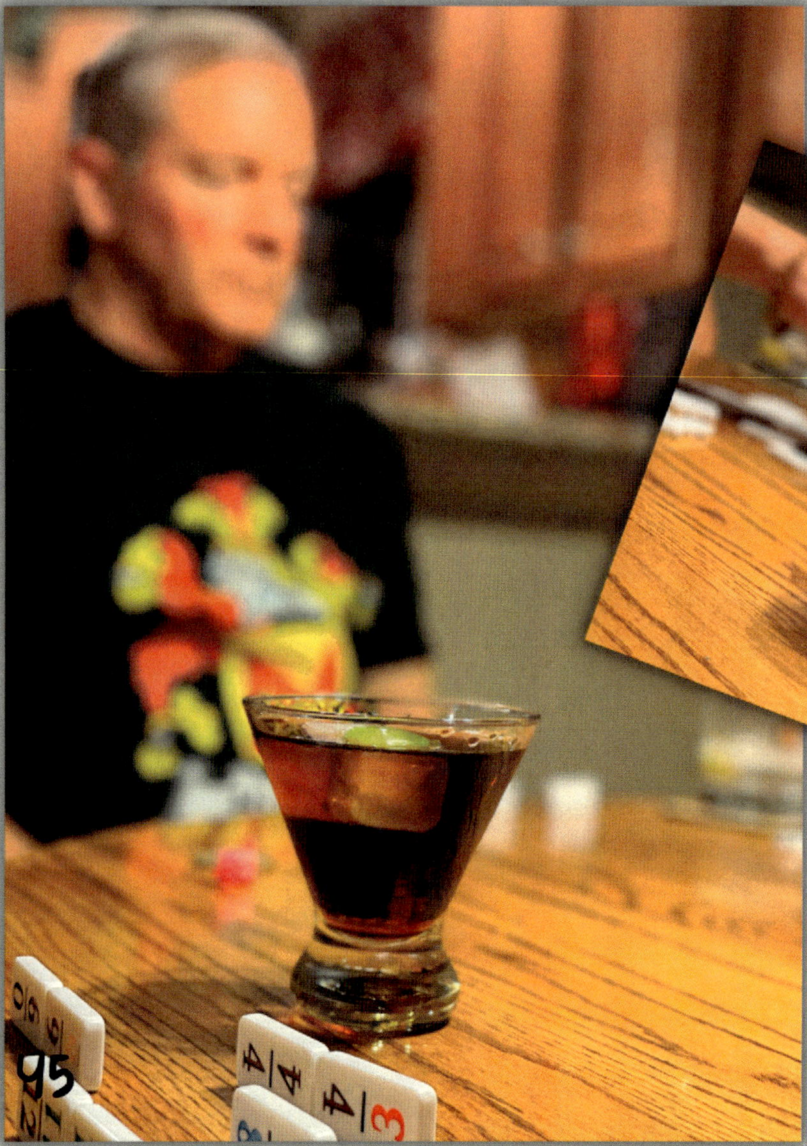

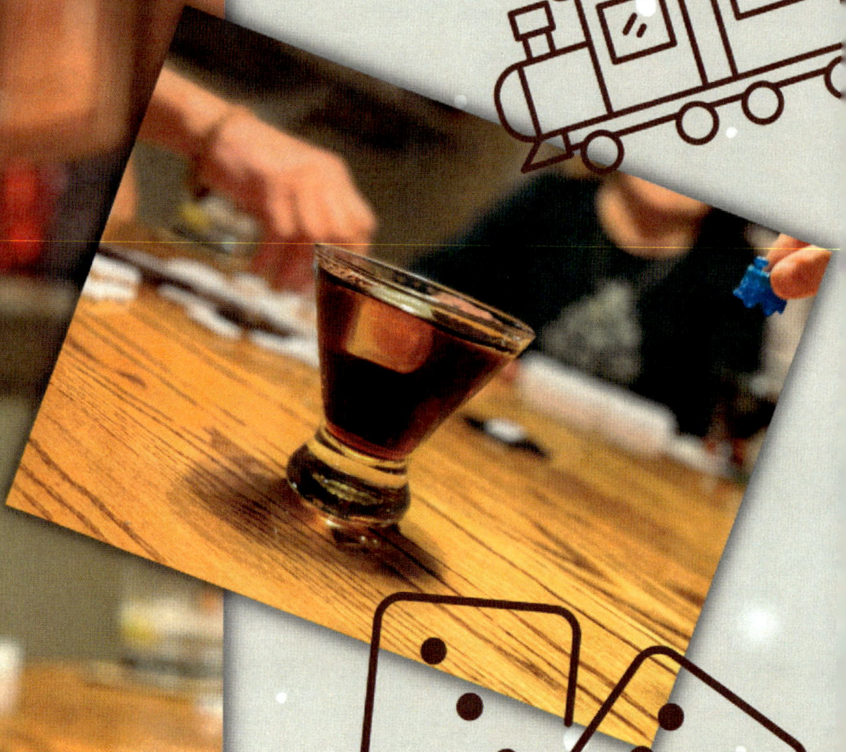

46

cheers!

48

49

*Love*

50

51

52

53

54

55

56

*family*

58

*family*

59

family

61

62

63

64

65

66

67

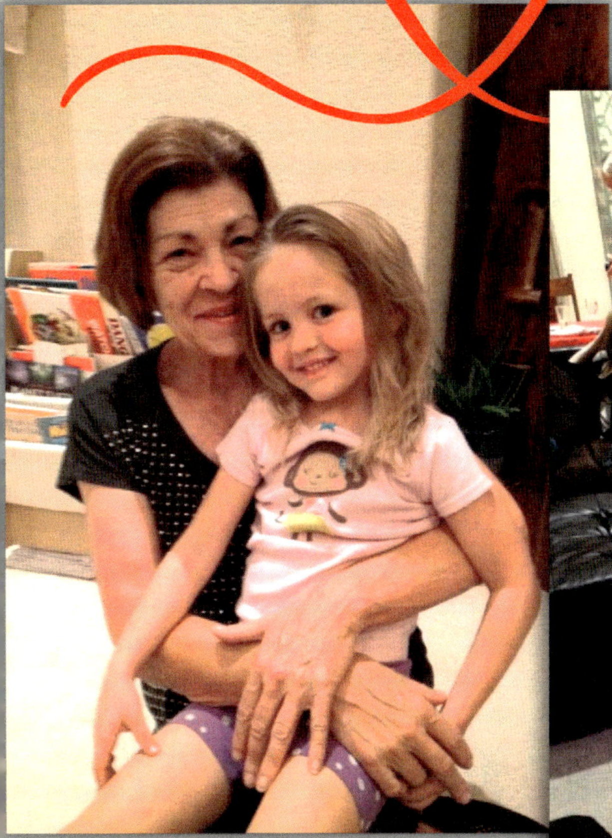

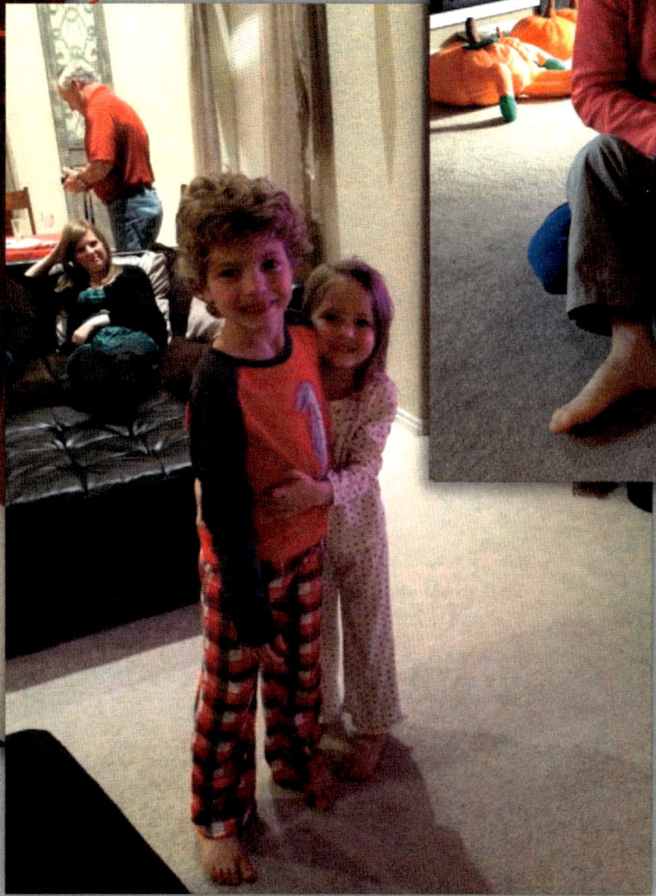

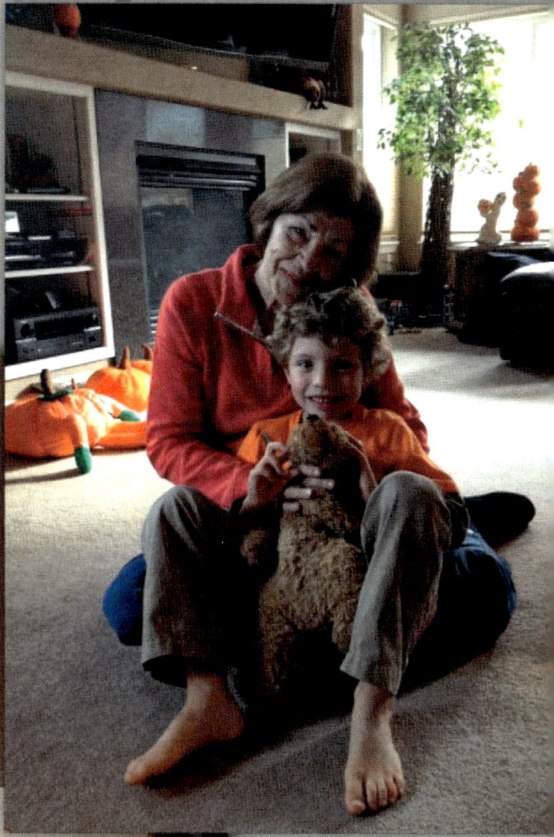

69

70

71

72

73

I MAY BE WRONG BUT I DOUBT IT

74

Made in the USA
Middletown, DE
28 May 2023